Children's Mass Book

This Book belongs to:

Madison Grace

Date _May 16, 2014_

When we eat this Bread and drink this
   Cup,
we proclaim your Death, O Lord,
until you come again.

CHILDREN'S MASS BOOK

By Rev. Basil Senger, O.S.B.

Explained and Simplified
for Young Children

_____

**With Official Text of People's Parts
of the Holy Mass**

In Accord with the Third Typical Edition
of the Roman Missal

CATHOLIC BOOK PUBLISHING CORP.
New Jersey

Nihil Obstat: Daniel V. Flynn, J.C.D.
Censor Librorum

Imprimatur: ✠ Joseph T. O'Keefe
Administrator, Archdiocese of New York

BLACK type for Responses said aloud
BLUE type for Explanations
RED type for Directions or Rubrics

(T-807)

ISBN 978-0-89942-807-9
CPSIA November 2011 10 9 8 7 6 5 4 3 2 1 A/P

© 2011, 1983 Catholic Book Publishing Corp., NJ
Printed in Hong Kong

To Parents and Teachers

THIS Children's Mass Book is a valuable aid for parents and teachers to introduce a child to the Mass.

This Mass Book gives the assistance that is considered most necessary for children. Directions are printed in red and explanations are printed in blue. Most important, all the responses which are said aloud are printed in bold black type.

The pictures . . . should attract the attention of the children, impress them, and gradually lead them to understand the actions and meaning of Holy Mass.

As soon as the children have become more familiar with the celebration of the Mass and can read the book themselves, they should be guided to the use of a more complete Missal and Hymnal.

Rev. Basil Senger, O.S.B.

INTRODUCTION

Jesus said:

**"Let the children come to me
and do not hinder them.
For the kingdom of God belongs to
such as these."**

Jesus the Savior of the world speaks.
He loves children.
He wants to be very near them.
He wants to bless them.
He wants to give them his love.

Jesus the Savior invites all of us to the
holy celebration of the Mass.

We are baptized children of God.
Therefore we ought to go to church
for the divine celebration.

Do everything that Jesus says.

Mary also gives us good advice:

One day Jesus was at a wedding in Cana.
His mother Mary and his disciples were also there.
The guests did not have any more wine.
No one knew what to do.
Only Mary believed that Jesus would help.
He did help: Jesus made water become wine.
By this he gave a sign of his glory.
At every celebration of Holy Mass
the Savior gives us precious wine:
His Sacred Blood that he shed on the Cross for us.

Give to the people to eat.

Once, when Jesus had announced
the Good News to the hungry people,
no one could feed them.
Then Jesus took some bread, gave thanks,
blessed it, broke it, and gave it to his disciples.
The disciples distributed it.
The people ate and everyone was satisfied.

At the celebration of the Mass,
the Priest on behalf of Christ speaks
the great prayer of thanks over the gifts.
Then the Body and Blood of Christ are
distributed to all.

THE ORDER OF MASS

THE INTRODUCTORY RITES

Entrance Chant   **STAND**

The congregation has assembled.
The Priest enters with the servers.
The Savior of the world calls us
to himself and to his sacrifice and meal.
He especially calls children, too.
We want to sing joyfully.

All make the Sign of the Cross:

Priest: In the name of the Father, and of
the Son, and of the Holy Spirit.

PEOPLE: Amen.

The Greeting

One of the following forms is used:
(Shown by A *,* B *, or* C *)*

A

Priest: The grace of our Lord Jesus Christ
   and the love of God,
and the communion of the Holy Spirit
be with you all.

PEOPLE: And with your spirit.

B ——————— OR ———————

Priest: Grace to you and peace from God
   our Father
and the Lord Jesus Christ.

PEOPLE: And with your spirit.

C ——————— OR ———————

Priest: The Lord be with you.

PEOPLE: And with your spirit.

The Penitential Act

We are invited to be sorry for our sins.

Priest: Brethren (brothers and sisters), let us acknowledge our sins,

and so prepare ourselves to celebrate the sacred mysteries.

Then one of the following A, B, or C forms is used.

A

Priest and PEOPLE:

I confess to almighty God
and to you, my brothers and sisters,
that I have greatly sinned,
in my thoughts and in my words,
in what I have done and in what I have failed to do,

And, striking their breast, they say:

through my fault, through my fault,
through my most grievous fault;

Then they continue:

therefore I ask blessed Mary ever-Virgin,
all the Angels and Saints,
and you, my brothers and sisters,
to pray for me to the Lord our God.

B ———————— OR ————————

Priest: Have mercy on us, O Lord.

PEOPLE: For we have sinned against you.

Priest: Show us, O Lord, your mercy.

PEOPLE: And grant us your salvation.

C ———————— OR ————————

Priest or other minister:

You were sent to heal the contrite of heart:

Lord, have mercy.

PEOPLE: Lord, have mercy.

Priest or other minister:

You came to call sinners:

Christ, have mercy.

PEOPLE: Christ, have mercy.

Priest or other minister:

You are seated at the right hand of the
Father to intercede for us:

Lord, have mercy.

PEOPLE: Lord, have mercy.

(Other invocations may be used.)

*At the end of any of the forms of the
Penitential Act is said:*

Priest: May almighty God have mercy on us,

forgive us our sins,

and bring us to everlasting life.

PEOPLE: Amen.

The Kyrie

(Except when Form C is used)

**We praise our Lord Jesus Christ
who loves us and wants to be merciful to us:**

Priest: Lord, have mercy.

PEOPLE: Lord, have mercy.

Priest: Christ, have mercy.

PEOPLE: Christ, have mercy.

Priest: Lord, have mercy.

PEOPLE: Lord, have mercy.

The Gloria (Hymn of Praise)

Glory to God in the highest,
and on earth peace to people of good will.
We praise you,
we bless you,
we adore you,
we glorify you,
we give you thanks for your great glory,
Lord God, heavenly King,
O God, almighty Father.

Lord Jesus Christ, Only Begotten Son,
Lord God, Lamb of God, Son of the Father,
you take away the sins of the world,
    have mercy on us;
you take away the sins of the world,
    receive our prayer;
you are seated at the right hand of the
    Father,
    have mercy on us.

For you alone are the Holy One,
you alone are the Lord,
you alone are the Most High,
Jesus Christ,
with the Holy Spirit,
in the glory of God the Father. Amen.

17

Collect

All the people, who have
come to the holy celebration of the Mass
form one family: the people of God.

We have assembled in the church,
in order to pray to the Father in heaven.
That is why the Savior is present among us.

The Priest raises his hands for prayer. Each Mass
has its own Collect.

Priest: Let us pray.

Grant, we pray, almighty God,
that your Church may always remain that
   holy people,
formed as one by the unity of Father, Son
   and Holy Spirit,
which manifests to the world
the Sacrament of your holiness and unity
and leads it to the perfection of your charity.
Through our Lord Jesus Christ, your Son,
who lives and reigns with you in the unity of
   the Holy Spirit,
one God, for ever and ever.

PEOPLE: Amen.

THE LITURGY OF THE WORD

SIT

First Reading

We hear what God wants to say through a prophet or apostle.
A lector proclaims the word of God.
We sit and listen.

At end of the reading:

Reader: The word of the Lord.
PEOPLE: Thanks be to God.

Responsorial Psalm

The people repeat the response after each verse.

Second Reading

At the end of the reading:

Reader: The word of the Lord.
PEOPLE: Thanks be to God.

21

The Gospel

STAND

The Savior himself speaks to us.
We stand and hear his word.

Deacon (or Priest):
The Lord be with you.

PEOPLE: And with your spirit.

Deacon (or Priest):
✠ A reading from the holy Gospel according to N.

PEOPLE: Glory to you, O Lord.

At the end:

Deacon (or Priest):
The Gospel of the Lord.

PEOPLE: Praise to you, Lord Jesus Christ.

The Priest explains the reading.

23

Profession of Faith (Creed)

STAND

All say the Profession of Faith on Sundays.

**I believe in one God
the Father almighty,
maker of heaven and earth,
of all things visible and invisible.**

**I believe in one Lord Jesus Christ,
the Only Begotten Son of God,
born of the Father before all ages.
God from God, Light from Light,
true God from true God,
begotten, not made, consubstantial with
   the Father;
through him all things were made.
For us men and for our salvation
he came down from heaven,**

*At the words that follow, up to and including
and became man, all bow.*

**and by the Holy Spirit was incarnate of the
   Virgin Mary,
and became man.**

For our sake he was crucified under
Pontius Pilate,
he suffered death and was buried,
and rose again on the third day
in accordance with the Scriptures.
He ascended into heaven
and is seated at the right hand of the
Father.
He will come again in glory
to judge the living and the dead
and his kingdom will have no end.

I believe in the Holy Spirit, the Lord, the
giver of life,
who proceeds from the Father and the
Son,
who with the Father and the Son is adored
and glorified,
who has spoken through the prophets.

I believe in one, holy, catholic and apos-
tolic Church.
I confess one Baptism for the forgiveness
of sins
and I look forward to the resurrection of
the dead
and the life of the world to come. Amen.

The Universal Prayer (Prayer of the Faithful)
We pray together with Christ to the Father in heaven for the Church and for all people.

Deacon or Reader:
Our response to each petition will be:
Lord, hear our prayer.

PEOPLE: Lord, hear our prayer.

For your holy Church.
For all who bear the responsibility for others.
For those who are starving and suffering.
For peace in this world.
For our whole congregation.
For all our families.
For fathers and mothers.
For our friends.
For all children and young people.
For the healthy and sick.
For the living and dead.

The Priest concludes with a prayer.

At the end:

PEOPLE: Amen.

SIT

27

LITURGY OF THE EUCHARIST

The Preparation of the Gifts

Water, wine, and bread are our gifts as a sign of our love and sacrificial offering with Christ. The Priest takes them and offers them to God.

Preparation of the Bread

Priest: Blessed are you, Lord God of all creation,
for through your goodness we have received
the bread we offer you:
fruit of the earth and work of human hands,
it will become for us the bread of life.

If there is no singing, the response is:

PEOPLE: Blessed be God for ever.

Preparation of the Wine

Priest: Blessed are you, Lord God of all creation,
for through your goodness we have received
the wine we offer you:
fruit of the vine and work of human hands,
it will become our spiritual drink.

It there is no singing, the response is:

PEOPLE: Blessed be God for ever.

Priest: Pray, brethren (brothers and sisters),
that my sacrifice and yours
may be acceptable to God,
the almighty Father.

STAND

PEOPLE: May the Lord accept the sacrifice at your hands
for the praise and glory of his name,
for our good
and the good of all his holy Church.

After a prayer by the Priest:

PEOPLE: Amen.

The Eucharistic Prayer

A prayer of praise and thanksgiving.

Priest: The Lord be with you.

PEOPLE: And with your spirit.

Priest: Lift up your hearts.

PEOPLE: We lift them up to the Lord.

Priest: Let us give thanks to the Lord our God.

PEOPLE: It is right and just.

The Priest says or sings a prayer that recalls one of the wonderful works God has done for us. It is called the Preface.

We all join in with our praise:

**Holy, Holy, Holy Lord God of hosts.
Heaven and earth are full of your glory.
Hosanna in the highest.
Blessed is he who comes in the name of the Lord.
Hosanna in the highest.   KNEEL**

The Priest continues to read the solemn prayer, and asks that the Father may sanctify the gifts:

Make holy, therefore, these gifts, we pray,
by sending down your Spirit upon them like the dewfall,
so that they become for us
the Body and ✠ Blood of our Lord Jesus Christ.

The same thing happens as in the Last Supper Room, when Jesus gave thanks over the bread and the chalice and said to his disciples:

Take this, all of you, and eat of it,
for this is my Body,
which will be given up for you.

In a similar way, when supper was ended,
he took the chalice
and, once more giving thanks,
he gave it to his disciples, saying:

Take this, all of you, and drink from it,
for this is the chalice of my Blood,
the Blood of the new and eternal covenant,
which will be poured out for you and for many
for the forgiveness of sins.

Do this in memory of me.

33

Memorial Acclamation

We look at the holy Bread and the chalice.

Priest: The mystery of faith.

PEOPLE: **We proclaim your Death, O Lord,**
A   **and profess your Resurrection**
    until you come again.

———————— OR ————————

B   **When we eat this Bread and**
    drink this Cup,

we proclaim your Death, O Lord,
until you come again.

—— OR ——

Save us, Savior of the world,
for by your Cross and Resurrection
you have set us free.

The Great "Amen"

When the Priest raises a little of
Christ's precious Blood in the chalice
together with his Body
we express that we want to praise,
honor, glorify, and thank the Father,
—through, with and in Christ.

Through him, and with him, and in him,
O God, almighty Father,
in the unity of the Holy Spirit,
all glory and honor is yours,
for ever and ever.

PEOPLE: Amen.

37

THE COMMUNION RITE

The Lord's Prayer

Jesus himself has taught us this prayer.
He is the life-giving Bread that the
Father gives us to nourish us.
The "Our Father" is the most beautiful
Communion prayer we can say.

STAND

**Our Father, who art in heaven,
hallowed be thy name;
thy kingdom come,
thy will be done
on earth as it is in heaven.
Give us this day our daily bread,
and forgive us our trespasses,
as we forgive those who trespass against
    us;
and lead us not into temptation,
but deliver us from evil.**

After another prayer of the Priest, the people say:

**For the kingdom,
the power and the glory are yours
now and for ever.**

Jesus and His Apostles at the Last Supper

Sign of Peace

We are God's children and guests at his table.
We are to receive his holy Body and Blood.
Before this we give the sign of peace
and we again pray for the mercy of the Lord.

Priest: For ever and ever.

PEOPLE: Amen.

Priest: The peace of the Lord be with you
   always.

PEOPLE: And with your spirit.

Deacon (or Priest):
   Let us offer each other the sign of peace.

PEOPLE:

**Lamb of God, you take away the sins of
   the world, / have mercy on us.**

**Lamb of God, you take away the sins of
   the world, / have mercy on us.**

**Lamb of God, you take away the sins of
   the world, / grant us peace.**

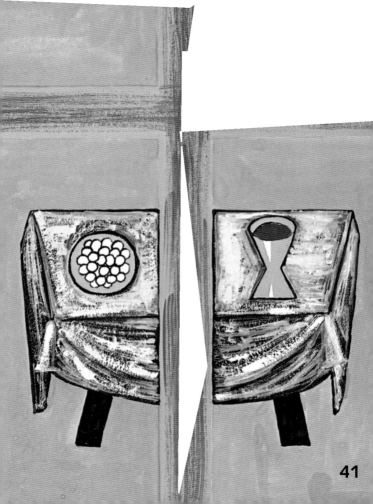

Communion

As Saint Peter said at the Last Supper,
when the Savior wanted to wash his feet—
and the centurion of Capernaum believed
in the greatness of the Lord—
so we want to say:

**Lord, I am not worthy
that you should enter under my roof,
but only say the word
and my soul shall be healed.**

All who participate at Holy Mass and are properly
disposed are called to receive Communion.

The Priest gives Communion to the people.

Priest: The Body of Christ:

Communicant: Amen.

Priest: The Blood of Christ.

Communicant: Amen.

We are as close to Jesus the Savior
as the Apostle John was at the Last Supper.
John rests on the breast of the Lord.
We unite ourselves with the love and sacrifice.

43

Communion Chant

The Communion Chant is sung while Communion is given to the faithful.

SIT

Silence after Communion

After Communion there may be a period of silence, or a song of praise may be sung.

Prayer after Communion

STAND

Priest: Let us pray.

Priest and people may pray silently for a while.

Then the Priest says the Prayer after Communion.

At the end:

Priest: Through Christ our Lord.

PEOPLE: Amen.

THE CONCLUDING RITES

We have heard God's word and
been nourished with Christ's Body and Blood.
Now, it is time for us to leave,
to do good works, to praise and bless the Lord
in our daily lives.

The Blessing

STAND

Priest: The Lord be with you.

PEOPLE: And with your spirit.

Priest: May almighty God bless you,
the Father, and the Son, ✠ and the Holy
Spirit.

PEOPLE: Amen.

Dismissal

Deacon (or Priest):

A Go forth, the Mass is ended.

——————— OR ———————

B Go and announce the Gospel of the Lord.

——————— OR ———————

C Go in peace, glorifying the Lord by your life.

——————— OR ———————

D Go in peace.

PEOPLE: Thanks be to God.

We leave the Church and return to our homes
and give life to the world.

Jesus said:
I have come that they may have life,
and have it in abundance. — *John 10:10*

OUR FATHER

OUR Father, . . . *as on page 38.*

HAIL MARY

HAIL Mary, full of grace
the Lord is with thee;
blessed art thou among women,
and blessed is the fruit of thy womb,
Jesus.
Holy Mary, Mother of God,
pray for us sinners,
now and at the hour of our death.
Amen.

PRAISE TO GOD

GLORY be to the Father,
and to the Son,
and to the Holy Spirit,
as it was in the beginning,
is now, and ever shall be,
world without end. Amen.